Level 5 – Green

Helpful Hints for Reading at Home

The graphemes (written letters) and phonemes (units of sound) used throughout this series are aligned with Letters and Sounds. This offers a consistent approach to learning, whether reading at home or in the classroom.

HERE IS A LIST OF NEW PHONEMES FOR THIS PHASE OF LEARNING. AN EXAMPLE OF THE PRONUNCIATION CAN BE FOUND IN BRACKETS.

Phase 5			
ay (day)	ou (out)	ie (tie)	ea (eat)
oy (boy)	ir (girl)	ue (blue)	aw (saw)
wh (when)	ph (photo)	ew (new)	oe (toe)
au (Paul)	a_e (make)	e_e (these)	i_e (like)
o_e (home)	u_e (rule)		

Phase 5 Alternative Pronunciations of Graphemes			
a (hat, what)	e (bed, she)	i (fin, find)	o (hot, so, other)
u (but, unit)	c (cat, cent)	g (got, giant)	ow (cow, blow)
ie (tied, field)	ea (eat, bread)	er (farmer, herb)	ch (chin, school, chef)
y (yes, by, very)	ou (out, shoulder, could, you)		

HERE ARE SOME WORDS WHICH YOUR CHILD MAY FIND TRICKY.

Phase 5 Tricky Words			
oh	their	people	Mr
Mrs	looked	called	asked
could			

TOP TIPS FOR HELPING YOUR CHILD TO READ:

- Allow children time to break down unfamiliar words into units of sound and then encourage children to string these sounds together to create the word.

- Encourage your child to point out any focus phonics when they are used.

- Read through the book more than once to grow confidence.

- Ask simple questions about the text to assess understanding.

- Encourage children to use illustrations as prompts.

This book focuses on /ey/ and is a Green level 5 book band.

How many words can you think of that have an ey sound?

Here are a few to get you started:

Key

Honey

Donkey

The key to a fun trip away is to plan things to see and do as you travel.

Turkey is an interesting spot to travel to. There are some things in Turkey that you must not miss.

Turkey is next to the sea. You can visit a Turkish beach as part of the trip.

Turkey has a lot of high hills, such as Mount Ararat. It has lots of valleys, too.

Mount Ararat

If you go to Pasabag Valley, you will see lots of rock chimneys in a cluster.

You might see hot air balloons near the chimneys. You could go in one to survey the chimneys from up high.

When you go, you will need to get Turkish coins. You can spend them at a market.

You can spend the coins on street food, too. You can get food, such as hot corn, from red trolleys.

Corn

In Mardin, donkeys help to keep the streets clean. They go up thin stairs and alleys that big trucks cannot.

Donkey

They are fed well with food such as barley.

Turkey has lots of interesting people and spots to visit.

There is too much to see in just one trip. You will have to go back to see it all!

©2023 **BookLife Publishing Ltd.**
King's Lynn, Norfolk, PE30 4LS, UK.

ISBN 978-1-80505-060-5

All rights reserved. Printed in China.
A catalogue record for this book is
available from the British Library.

Turkey
Written by Charis Mather
Designed by Isabella Croker

An Introduction to BookLife Readers...

Our Readers have been specifically created in line with the London Institute of Education's approach to book banding and are phonetically decodable and ordered to support each phase of the Letters and Sounds document.

Each book has been created to provide the best possible reading and learning experience. Our aim is to share our love of books with children, providing both emerging readers and prolific page-turners with beautiful books that are guaranteed to provoke interest and learning, regardless of ability.

BOOK BAND GRADED using the Institute of Education's approach to levelling.

PHONETICALLY DECODABLE supporting each phase of Letters and Sounds.

EXERCISES AND QUESTIONS to offer reinforcement and to ascertain comprehension.

CLEAR DESIGN to inspire and provoke engagement, providing the reader with clear visual representations of each non-fiction topic.

AUTHOR INSIGHT:
CHARIS MATHER

Charis Mather is a children's author at BookLife Publishing who has a love for reading and writing. Her studies in linguistics and experiences working with young readers have given her a knack for writing material that suits a range of ages and skill levels. Charis is passionate about producing books that emphasise the fun in reading and is convinced that no matter how much you already know, there is always something new to learn.

PHASE 5
/ey/

This book focuses on /ey/ and is a Green level 5 book band.

Image Credits Images are courtesy of Shutterstock.com. With thanks to Getty Images, Thinkstock Photo and iStockphoto.
Cover – topseller, Marti Bug Catcher, Carmian. 3 – Rosa Jay, Dionisvera, AlexGreenArt. 4–5 – Seqoya, Prostock-studio. 6–7 – MehmetO, Hakan Tanak. 8–9 – DreamStoreCo, Nick N A. 10–11 – alexfan32, SergeyKPI. 12–13 – Giancarlo Polacchini, Tehsin Baravi. 14–15 – Olena Yakobchuk, frantic00.